Somerset

Edited By Brixie Payne

First published in Great Britain in 2019 by:

 Young**Writers**®
— Est. 1991 —

Young Writers
Remus House
Coltsfoot Drive
Peterborough
PE2 9BF
Telephone: 01733 890066
Website: www.youngwriters.co.uk

FOREWORD

Here at Young Writers, we love to let imaginations run wild and creativity go crazy. Our aim is to encourage young people to get their creative juices flowing and put pen to paper. Each competition is tailored to the relevant age group, hopefully giving each pupil the inspiration and incentive to create their own piece of creative writing, whether it's a poem or a short story. By allowing them to see their own work in print, we know their confidence and love for the written word will grow.

For our latest competition Poetry Wonderland, we invited primary school pupils to create wild and wonderful poems on any topic they liked – the only limits were the limits of their imagination! Using poetry as their magic wand, these young poets have conjured up worlds, creatures and situations that will amaze and astound or scare and startle! Using a variety of poetic forms of their own choosing, they have allowed us to get a glimpse into their vivid imaginations. We hope you enjoy wandering through the wonders of this book as much as we have.

CONTENTS

Hannah Power (10)	60
James Adams (10)	61
Roxanne Wylie (10)	62
Zuzanna Jaroni (10)	64
Ola Kopyto (10)	65
Maxine Lampard (10)	66
Nadia Bohdan (9)	67
Lewis Williams (10)	68
Bethany Barnett (10)	69
Daniel David Colohan (9)	70
Edward Cutts (9)	71
Zachary Palmer (9)	72
Tomas Sims (10)	73
Joshua Ruppersbery (9)	74
Olivier Piatek (10)	75
Sergio Manuel Maleiro (10)	76
Katie Berry (9)	77
Filip Wasyleczko (9)	78

Somerset Bridge Primary School, Bridgwater

Caitlin Price (10)	79
Maizie-May Conway (10)	80
Ruby Elizabeth Boobyer (10)	82
Sadie McSweeney-Stevens (10)	84
Flynn Stuckey (10)	85
Gracjan Kapral (10)	86
Jack Turner (10)	87
Casey Pester (10)	88
Mia Charlotte Hawkins (10)	89
Sophia Heal (10)	90
Tilly Stevens (10)	91
Jessica Knight (11)	92
Lilly-Ann Weaver (10)	93
Toby Larwood (10)	94
Lorelei Murdoch (10)	95
Aaron Bojko (10)	96
Grace Payne (10)	97
Cynthia Sosnowska (10)	98
Libby Coupland (11)	99
Charlie Coles (10)	100
Jenna Frances Lyddon-Roberts (10)	101

Kieran Upham (11)	102
Naomi Wiacek (10)	103
Millie Doughty (11)	104

St Michael's Academy, Yeovil

Daniel Linsdell (8)	105
Troy Ford (7)	106
Lucas Conway (7)	107

St Philip's CE Primary School, Odd Down

Sophie Webb (9)	108
Cara Willcox (7)	109
Ben McLaughlan (9)	110
Nathan Saji John (10)	112
Todd Clay (10)	114
Gracie Williams (8)	115
Jasper Richardson (11)	116
Lilly Dyer (9)	118
Charlie Williams (8)	119
Tia Jovanovska (7)	120
Charlie Pym (10)	121
Samuel James Kindon (9)	122
Robbie Skellern (10)	123
Emmy Habgood (7)	124
Oliver Hutchings (9)	125
Harry Williams (10)	126
Daisy Ann Gregory (7)	127
Matthew Bradley (7)	128
Eleanor May Favager (10)	129
Jayden Draper (9)	130
Riley Prior (9)	132
Ethan O'Connor (10)	133
Reuben John Waldron (9)	134
Harry Houldsworth (10)	135
Corina Franklin (7)	136
Bun Li (7)	137
Joel Atkinson (10)	138
Ava Parry-Smith (9)	139
Faith Adeline Baldeo (10)	140
Joshua Alan Scarrott (8)	141
Ivy Yang (8)	142

Eryn Higgins (10)	143
Ruby Grace Favager (8)	144
Oliver James Holt (10)	145
Libby Mason (8)	146
Harry Hall (11)	147
Chloe Pym (8)	148
Ryan Fender (7)	149
Oscar Costello (10)	150
Shay Lewis (9)	152
Amelia May Hargreaves (8)	153
Ezra Banham (9)	154
Elijah Baggan (7)	155
Corey Summers (9)	156
Sophie Mitchell (8)	157
Willis Skardon (10)	158
Maya Nascimento (10)	159
Ruby Treweek (8)	160
Connor Snelling (10)	161
Cheyenne Moyle (9)	162
Morgan Currie (8)	163
Luke Thompson (10)	164
Nancy Costa Cupe (7)	165
Tia Louise Watts (7)	166
Sophie Holborn (8)	167
Zach Turner (7)	168
Lewis James Mitchell (7)	169
Louis Knight (9)	170
Sara Maria Faur (9)	171
Emmanuelle Maria Sasarman (7)	172
Calum Willcox (9)	173
Liam John Quintin (10)	174
Taliah Kathryn Johnson (10)	175
Amelia Offler (7)	176
Eden Lawbuary-Stock (7)	177
Sofia Mutlow (7)	178
William McIvor (8)	179
Riley Joyce (8)	180
Max Lakey (7)	181
Molly Coles (8)	182
Juliet Usher (8)	183
Tayla Ward (8)	184

Voyage Learning Campus, Worle

Amelia Dewey (10)	185
Rhys Murphy (11)	186
Harley Pearce (10)	187
Harmony Reed (11)	188
Jayden Boyd (10)	189
Toby Williams (8)	190
Kyros Alabaf (9)	191
Rhys Jefferies (9)	192
Harry Dobbing (9)	193
James Pearce (10)	194

Weston All Saints Primary School, Weston

Romilly C (10)	195
Lydia Shearman (11)	196
Reilly M (10)	198
Edward H (10)	199
Mohima C (10)	200
Jack Cartwright (10)	201
Andrew Docton (10)	202

THE POEMS

Dragons

Dragon, dragon where could you be?
In a cave or up a tree?
Are you red? Are you green?
Are you a myth? Have you ever been seen?
In my book, you're up a tower,
Guarding treasure with your fire power,
Keeping the princess safe from scary things,
Flying away with your giant wings,
Getting into sword fights,
Slashing your sword and doing some damage,
Lord Dragon, I wish you were real,
Please just come here, I'll be your friend and that's
a deal.

Harrison E Izzard (7)
Axbridge CE First School, Axbridge

Rugby Life

First thing on Sunday, rugby begins,
Socks pulled up, boots done tight,
We are almost ready for our fight.

We go to our huddle,
I stand in the middle,
We put our hands together,
And shout, "Weston forever!"

We form our defensive line,
The whistle goes,
We run in time.

Snatching tag after tag,
Slipping and sliding,
Boots gripping and gliding,
Another tag in the bag.

Tries are scored,
Conversions are kicked,
Fingers are broken,
Noses are squished.

Thank God it's not football,
The game would be off,
Ref's out of puff,
Mum's cold and stormed off in a huff.

The whistle is blown,
No one's the winner,
Don't worry, off to the club for dinner.

Hands are shaken,
Friends are made,
Dad's got a beer,
He says it's lemonade.

Rugby's not just a game,
It's part of my life!
I'll play it forever,
Or until I have a wife.

Reuben Corbett (7)
Axbridge CE First School, Axbridge

Ice Cream Dreams!

Ice cream, ice cream,
Come to me,
With your tasty treats and sweets to eat,
Juicy lollies and chocolate sprinkles,
Strawberry and vanilla ice cream cones,
All the yummy things I think of,
When I hear your music tinkle,
Ice cream, ice cream,
Cold and wet,
In my belly you must get!
Mr Whippy, 99 Flakes or Screwballs,
I don't mind,
Ice cream, I love you!

Poppy Johnson (7)
Axbridge CE First School, Axbridge

Ocean Danger

I once made friends with a fish,
it would taste lovely on a dish.
But there was an undersea volcano meltdown,
sadly, my fish got knocked right down.

Then I made friends with a shark,
but his slimy scales were too sharp.
A fisherman came,
he took my shark away - I took the blame.

After that, I made friends with a dolphin,
the problem was, it had no fin!
Then there was a flood,
my dolphin drowned and there was blood.

Before you get in the ocean,
put on suntan lotion!
And remember, strangers...
in the ocean there are many dangers.

Ella Anstice (9)
Bishop Henderson CE Primary School, Taunton

The Alien That Came To Taunton

Now, I'm pretty sure,
you've never seen anything as ugly before,
now close your eyes,
you're in for a surprise,
his name is Bog,
and he looks like a frog,
his teeth are green,
they could do with a clean,
his eyes are as wide,
as the incoming tide,
his breath's so vile,
you could smell it from a mile,
he came to Taunton on a flying mat,
singing like a strangled cat,
he landed on the roof,
and went down the chimney with a poof,
then he decided to have some fun,
so he played pranks on everyone,
he put slime in the loo,

broke the table in two,
turned all their food into a stew,
with all the mischief done,
off Bog flew into the sun.

Madison Burton (10)

Bishop Henderson CE Primary School, Taunton

The Magic Box

Inspired by 'The Magic Box' by Kit Wright

I will put into the box...
The first song of a whale
The first berries of the earth
The last ocean
The last tears of a dragon
The smell of the morning dew
The swish of blossom
The song of a nightingale
The sound of a waterfall
The yap of a puppy
The sight of silver dolphins
The deep feeling of my heart
The friendship of the world
My box is made of secrets, sunlight and water
My box has animal patterns engraved on it
The hinges on my box are the spirits of the earth.

Freya Margrett (8)

Bishop Henderson CE Primary School, Taunton

The Great Escape From London Zoo

The great escape from London Zoo
All the pandas abandoned their bamboo
Then they dressed up as railway crew
And drove away to Kathmandu
But ended up in north Peru
Then the humans thought that was a hullabaloo
And then all the pandas laughed and said,
"Chickabubu!"
Then they got on train number twenty-two
Then they said, "We got on the wrong train, we
need forty-two!"
The great escape from London Zoo
The end of the pandas' hullabaloo.

Isla Melhuish (8)
Bishop Henderson CE Primary School, Taunton

Hide-And-Seek Went Weird!

My friends were running into every room,
This was not the game I'd planned!
My friends were like kangaroos,
Jumping on their hands.
I said, "It's time to play hide-and-seek!"
So my friends went to hide in the same spot,
But then they found a giant mouse hole,
They were all scared, so they teleported over me,
the seeker,
The seeker went in first,
And then everyone else followed,
We were all really scared,
Because we saw a big bad mouse!
We tried to run back,
But the mouse hole had shrunk,
And we could not fit back through!
But actually, the big bad mouse was just a normal
mouse,
It's just that everyone was tiny!

Ebony-mae French (7)
Bishops Hull Primary School, Bishops Hull

Living In A Whiteboard

Living in a whiteboard,
is not a lot of fun,
people keep writing,
which is very unfun.
There's no food to eat like a bun,
and you can't get out.
I'm all pink and green, all sorts of colours,
I can't rub it off, there's nothing to do it with.
There's nowhere to sleep because it's,
a squash and a squeeze.
It's not very harmful,
but there's not a lot to do,
there's not even a grill!
It's very grubby,
lots of gruesome stuff,
so come on everybody, join the non-fun house!

Eloise Catherine Reed (7)
Bishops Hull Primary School, Bishops Hull

The Day The Cheetah Followed Me

When I found a cheetah
that's when my day began
when I went to the park
I ran and ran
and it followed me
and I didn't like it, so
I went on the swings
and it ran to me
it chased me and chased me
for an hour and a half
I had a stitch that night
I didn't have tea
because the cheetah ate it instead
I brushed my teeth
and had a shower
and went straight to bed.
The next morning, I said,
"Magnificent!"
because the cheetah was gone!

Florence Griffiths (7)
Bishops Hull Primary School, Bishops Hull

Flower Bed

Tiny from that carrot, I now had small legs,
chasing the rabbit into a flower bed.
I heard a voice, I thought something was messing
with my head,
I thought, *no, flowers can't talk.*
"Well, we can talk,
but we can't walk,
we can sing too!"
I said, "Oh, please do!"
So they sang their song,
all day long,
and they liked singing it in June,
it was May and June was soon.
I realised I had to leave,
so I floated away like a leaf.

Isabelle Hawkins (11)
Bishops Hull Primary School, Bishops Hull

Babysitting Dragons

I was babysitting dragons and it went wrong.
They were...
Noisy,
Crazy,
Weird.

They...
Spat,
And kicked,
Until they went up to have a little nap.

When they woke up, they...
Ran out of the door into Rubber Land.
They saw another door and went through it.
They saw a cow and jumped on it.

They were...
Excited,
Screaming,
Funny,
Hungry,

Until I found them and gave them back to their parents.
It was a hard day!

Seren Marie Vickery (7)

Bishops Hull Primary School, Bishops Hull

A Trip To The Stars

One unusual morning,
I jumped out of bed,
and saw a scared lion.

With a grin, he asked,
"Do you need a lift?"
I said, "Yes please!"

I climbed on his back,
and he jumped through the window.
We shot into space,
and all I could see were stars.

Suddenly, a group of aliens,
asked if we could play football.
I said, "No."

Next, we went flying,
on shiny stars...

Mohamad Alewy Zedahy (9)
Bishops Hull Primary School, Bishops Hull

Riding A Horse Backwards

A lady travelled to a farm,
The farmer asked,
"Do you want to ride the horse?"
"Yes please!"
Said the lady.
So she got ready to ride the horse,
And the farmer left her with a step,
So she climbed onto the horse.
Before she could sit forwards,
The horse ran off,
The horse sped off,
Into a cave.
The lady fell off the horse,
And soon they were asleep.
Zzz...

Amelie Cox (7)
Bishops Hull Primary School, Bishops Hull

Riding A Hamster

My pet hamster is called Cinnamon,
She is very fluffy and adventurous,
One day, she said to me,
"Do you want to go on an adventure?"
I said, "Yes please!"
So I jumped onto her back and off we went,
We started flying into space,
When we landed, we found a land full of sweets,
We needed to explore,
There were planets made of sweets,
After that, we went to dig,
Then we went home.

Jasmine Inder (7)
Bishops Hull Primary School, Bishops Hull

The Girl Going To Places

I was jumping on the moon
with a big bad wolf
and there were flowers on the moon
and we were jumping like crazy.
I walked up to the farm
and I was walking with a cow and a mouse.
I was riding a tree,
then I was playing on the tree.
I was playing snowball fights with the cat, Park Lee
and the dog, Tom
and we were playing in the front garden.

Kara Whittle (7)

Bishops Hull Primary School, Bishops Hull

A Really Shiny Cookie

I found a shiny cookie
and ate it all up
and felt really weird
and turned really small
I saw myself
I was a pig!
I found a castle
it wasn't a usual one
it was colourful and shiny
and I laughed my head off
I had to get out
but the door was locked
wait, there were a billion doors
I couldn't believe my eyes...

Jack Mills (7)
Bishops Hull Primary School, Bishops Hull

Bouncing On The Moon

Bouncing on the moon with a cup of tea too
and then an alien wanted to join
I said, "Yes!"
Bouncing on the moon with an alien too
and a dragon asked if he could join
we said, "Yes!"
Bouncing on the moon with an alien too
with a dragon behind
then a monster wanted to join
we said...
"Run!"

Brooke James (10)
Bishops Hull Primary School, Bishops Hull

The Dream

I took a yummy picnic on a unicorn
All of it fell off
So I fell asleep
But it threw me off!

Then I landed in a cotton candy bed
It was all cosy and warm and fluffy.

I loved it in the bed
But when I woke up
I was back at home.

It must've been a dream
Or I'd floated off back home.

Jay Newton (7)
Bishops Hull Primary School, Bishops Hull

Sunbathing On The Sun

I was sunbathing on the sun and
felt like I was melting with lightness
I started to be white
upside down
it was round and rolling
I didn't know what to do
so I just called Pizza Hut
then they came
but when they delivered my pizza
I opened it
and there was nothing in there
so I went home.

Bobby Beattie (7)
Bishops Hull Primary School, Bishops Hull

Rainbow Stands For...

The red stands for love!
The orange stands for fire!
Yellow stands for sunlight!
The green stands for grass!
Blue stands for waves!
The turquoise stands for a beautiful eye colour!
Pink stands for cute cheeks!
Purple, black and white stand for the galaxy!
I wish all these colours were in a rainbow!

Laura Al-Guwary (10)
Bishops Hull Primary School, Bishops Hull

A Cat Driving A Tractor

One day, I went outside
And found a cat on a tractor
It was crazy, spectacular, funny
So I went over and the cat said, "Miaow!"

One day, there were animals
They went to the shop
The man in there was surprised what had happened
So the man jumped out the window in shock!

Harry Foxwell (7)
Bishops Hull Primary School, Bishops Hull

Play Tag With A Cheetah

Playing tag with a cheetah must be hard
Even when you get used to it, you'll still be last
The cheetah will win yet again
So why don't you try riding a hen?
If you win
You might get a bin
But really the cheetah won
So you pong
When you run
You'll just get a bun.

Scarlett Thorne (7)
Bishops Hull Primary School, Bishops Hull

A Pug Flying

I found a cute pug,
On a magical, mystical dragon,
In a dark and spooky cave,
The pug looked joyful,
When they came out,
The pug stole my sausage roll,
They soared past houses,
Stealing all the yummy sausages,
When they were back,
They had a great big snooze.

Jacob Staddon (8)

Bishops Hull Primary School, Bishops Hull

A Candy Day

I looked out the window,
out the window,
I saw some candy, candyfloss and chocolate.
When I was walking
I tamed a bunny
not just any bunny
a gummy bunny.
I had a nice swim
in the chocolate lake.
I got some milk
and sunbathed on a candyfloss cloud.

Imogen Setherton (7)
Bishops Hull Primary School, Bishops Hull

The Wonderland Rainbow

I see the red in a ruby
The orange in a fire
The yellow in the sunlight
And the green in the grass.

I see the blue in the sky
The purple of the night sky
The pink at dusk
And the black in coal.

There are lovely colours everywhere you look.

Elissa Rickard (10)
Bishops Hull Primary School, Bishops Hull

Miss Chicken

I went to the farm one day,
and saw a chicken along the way.
The chicken showed me how to lay eggs,
I said, "Great, let's go!"
So we went to the farmyard,
I managed to lay an egg.
I went home after my busy day,
I said, "Goodnight."

Eliza Grace Ford (7)
Bishops Hull Primary School, Bishops Hull

A Pug In Water

I found a pug in water
but it got onto a
crocodile.
The pug stole my chicken leg
and swam off
with my chicken leg.
I chased it until the swamp was no more
but the pug just wanted to be loved
and to have a home.

Eloise Johnson (7)
Bishops Hull Primary School, Bishops Hull

A Cat Played Hopscotch With A Dragon

A cat played hopscotch with a dragon...
the cave ground was shaking,
the roof was crumbling,
the ground was quaking,
the walls were falling,
the whole cave was trembling,
all because a dragon was playing hopscotch.

Freyja Elizabeth Petty (7)
Bishops Hull Primary School, Bishops Hull

A Unicorn At Sea

I saw a unicorn
her dream was to go to space
and her dream came true.
She went to the blue planet
she swam and
she came to the moon
and put her flag
on the moon.

Felicity Tiley (7)
Bishops Hull Primary School, Bishops Hull

Grandma's Going On Holiday

Grandma's going on holiday
Flying higher than the moon
And with her fast sprouting wings
She'll be back from her adventures soon
She writes to us about the trip
The Tart Mahal, the Empire Steak
Eating all the food is a big mistake
She eats the Leaning Tower of Pizza
And she grows so fat that from space you can see
her
It's no more fun, now she's on the run
From the police trying to shoot her bum
Photographers stand with open lips
Thinking she's a solar eclipse
Grandma flies until her chest is wheezy
Then spotting the Omoo Arena makes her queasy
All that dripping, yummy milk
Makes her sick on her jumper made of silk
She races back home and what's on the telly?
The news reporter talking about the food in her
belly,

"The Empire Steak has disappeared!"
Gulp! Everyone will think that's weird!
Then she gets the BBC's text...
'Which landmark are you gonna eat next?'
So Grandma's holiday hasn't been the best
Hopefully, it will be better after some rest.

Fraya Evans (10)

Charlton Mackrell CE Primary School, Charlton Mackrell

Granny's Poo

We go to Granny's house
She says, "It's nearly dinner."
We run and hide
But she finds us
We say, "Granny, we don't want to eat your poo!"
"Well you have to,"
Says Granny
Two days later, our mum gets near
But two weeks later, we have to go back
We scream and shout
And beg our mum to not
Let us go back
We try to get all of the
Granny poo out of our teeth
It's finally night, but
Granny's poo is haunting us.

Isobel Carrick (8)
Charlton Mackrell CE Primary School, Charlton Mackrell

The Exploding Chicken

Once there was a man called Bob
He ate so much, he was like a blob
Bob was out in the forest with trees
He turned around and began to freeze
An exploding chicken is what he saw
Next to him was a scary boar
He jumped into the river and swam away
Now the chicken began to play
It picked Bob up like a little feather
Underneath him was a patch of heather
He wiggled out and got back down
Bob thought that he deserved a crown
Then Bob was squished by a flying bed
From that point on, Bob was dead.

Alfie Carey (10)
Charlton Mackrell CE Primary School, Charlton Mackrell

The One-Million-Year-Old Granny

A one-million-year-old granny poisoning the moon
A one-million-year-old granny killing aliens with her farts
Wrinkly granny
Ugly granny
Even a little pimple-filled granny
Gross granny
Smelly granny
Why don't you take a bath, Granny?
Yucky granny
Poisonous granny
Gangster granny
Oh my goodness Granny
I'm fed up with Granny
Why don't you leave, big old Granny?
Oh my goodness, she is a crazy granny.

Chelsea David (11)
Charlton Mackrell CE Primary School, Charlton Mackrell

Pumpkin Playing Fortnite

Pumpkin playing Fortnite
He always lands in Wailing Woods
Pumpkin playing Fortnite
The first chest gives him an epic scar

Pumpkin playing Fortnite
Hear the pumpkin shout, he just lost health
Pumpkin playing Fortnite
See his pickaxe swing to get wood

Pumpkin playing Fortnite
He's in Dusty Depot now, he's going to win
Pumpkin playing Fortnite
Pat the pumpkin well done, he's won.

Amelia Light (10)
Charlton Mackrell CE Primary School, Charlton Mackrell

Giant Fish

Go, go, go to the pet shop
In the car we get
"Are we there?" I shout
"Not yet!"
"Are we now?"
The pet shop is round the corner

"Fish!" I shout. "I want a fish!"
Inside the pet shop we go
"Shh!" the owner says. "The animals are asleep."
"Here!" I whisper
I point to a giant, gold, sparkly fish!

Scarlet Adams (8)
Charlton Mackrell CE Primary School, Charlton Mackrell

Crazy Potato Family

Little Potato's birthday has arrived
Evil Potato is just coming by
Big Potato is on the run
Little Potato is having fun
Baby Potato is tucked up in bed
The twin potatoes are cuddling their teds
Mummy Potato is making dinner
Evil Potato thinks he's the winner
Little Potato screams for help
While Daddy Potato puts on his belt
Big Potato hears the screams
Mummy Potato finishes her beans
Daddy Potato goes to run
Evil Potato actually hasn't won
All potatoes now live in peace
Happy together, not even a peep!

Winnie Bess Carmichael (10)
Charlton Mackrell CE Primary School, Charlton Mackrell

Giant Potatoes Taking Over The World

Giant potatoes are coming
to towns,
Giant potatoes acting
as clowns,
Giant potatoes don't make
a sound,
Giant potatoes are very
round,
Giant potatoes have
massive hands,
Giant potatoes are going to take
over the world and the lands.

Jemima Carrick (10)
Charlton Mackrell CE Primary School, Charlton Mackrell

Octopus Travels

Flying to London on an octopus
Crashing into the moon
Falling back to Earth
Smashing into vehicles
Breaking houses down
Injuring my bones
Slipping off the octopus' head
Feeling slime on my arm
Smelling disgusting seawater
Falling down on people's heads
The octopus is tired, we land back in the sea
Holding my breath for a very long time
Bouncing onto coral
Drinking seawater
Slipping off the octopus
Holding his tentacle tight.

Casie-Jade Chubb (9)

Charlton Mackrell CE Primary School, Charlton Mackrell

Donkey Dance

D onkey dancers dancing to the beat
O n the black and white stage
N ot shaking their feet
K arl the donkey
E den the donkey
Y any the donkey

D onkey dancers are everywhere
A pples are the donkeys' favourite
N ot the core and stick though
C arol the donkey is listening to her rock music
E veryone's favourite is Drake's new track.

Eden Burke (8)

Charlton Mackrell CE Primary School, Charlton Mackrell

Going To London On An Octopus

Going to London on an octopus
Got me so sticky, slimy and slippery
Going to London on an octopus
Made me fall twenty times
Going to London on an octopus
Got me crashing into vehicles
Going to London on an octopus
Got me breaking big bulky houses down.

Imogen Grace Baker (10)
Charlton Mackrell CE Primary School, Charlton Mackrell

Toilet Trouble

I'm having a chat with Charles Xavier
And he goes to use the toilet
He searches for it and it is found
He opens the door and behold...
It's Wolverine doing the Orange Justice
Blowing huge bubbles with his claws out on the loo!
Hope this doesn't happen to you!

Kaiden James Allen (9)
Charlton Mackrell CE Primary School, Charlton Mackrell

The Vomiting Cat

The vomiting cat sat on the mat
The vomiting cat threw up its owner's hat
Its hairy exploding warts
The scary popping sound
The weary eyes
The glary grin
The marmalade ears
The whiskery chin
The shy eyes
The dimpled nose
The vomiting cat with the exploding hair warts is
coming for you!
So watch out because if you're not careful, you will
be next!

Evie Burrell (11)
Charlton Mackrell CE Primary School, Charlton Mackrell

Killer Eyeball

Killer Eyeball
Went to town
Killer Eyeball
Wanted the sparkly crown
Killer Eyeball
Would destroy anything in his way
Killer Eyeball
Shot his gooey goo
Killer Eyeball
Ate the people
Killer Eyeball
Met Hero Ear
Killer Eyeball
Struck Hero Ear
Killer Eyeball
Got the sparkly crown.

Peter Robinson O'Boyle (10)
Charlton Mackrell CE Primary School, Charlton Mackrell

Bad Babies

Babies taking over the world,
Shouting, "Bunewe chu nu begog begog!"
Shooting you with milk bottles,
Babies taking over the world,
Threatening to run you over with their prams,
Jump over walls,
No matter what you do, they'll stink you out.

George Chevis (9)
Charlton Mackrell CE Primary School, Charlton Mackrell

Dancing With A Jellyfish

Dancing with a jellyfish
didn't go as planned
I kept getting electric
shocks
My feet slipped on the
slimy floor
My hair was all stuck up
on end
I couldn't keep up with
the dancing anymore
So I decided to
slip away.

David Fraser (9)
Charlton Mackrell CE Primary School, Charlton Mackrell

Swimming In A Mouldy Chocolate Lake

Swimming in a mouldy lake didn't go as planned...
I got mould in my mouth
Chocolate on my clothes
My hair stuck to my back
I was as sticky as fudge
I was furry and mouldy
Eurgh gross! I would never do it again.

Matilda Stothard (9)

Charlton Mackrell CE Primary School, Charlton Mackrell

The Surfing Cat On The Rainbow

R iding on the colours
A bove the clouds
I diot cats riding on surfboards
N oisy miaowing
B obbing up and down
O n the bright bridge
W ow oh wow.

Sam Butler (9)

Charlton Mackrell CE Primary School, Charlton Mackrell

Men Riding Bikes On The Moon

Riding bikes
Starting bikes
Pushing bikes
Flying bikes
Smelly bikes
Fast bikes
Engines dying
Spaceships flying
To save people down below.

Luke Beckey (9)
Charlton Mackrell CE Primary School, Charlton Mackrell

Great, YouTubers Again

G reat YouTubers are usually funny,

R eally, lots are hilarious,

E ating the philosopher's stone (like Guava Juice) is stupid,

A li-A tries beating Godzilla at netball,

T ry if you want, but no one can beat Godzilla!

Y ouTubers do random videos,

O nly they know what they will do,

U nlimited YouTubers on YouTube,

'T ry not to laughs' are my favourite,

U ltimate ones (of course),

B eating me is easy, as I always lose,

E very video is unique,

R emember, DanTDM flies over active volcanoes on lightning bolts,

S o much silliness.

A nyone can be one, just believe,

G ood thing lots are funny,

A bout another 1000 videos were just made,

I love watching YouTube,
N ever going to stop!

James Bishop (10)
Our Lady Of Mount Carmel Catholic Primary School, Tout Hill

The Washing Monster

The soapy, slimy, rhyming washing monster,
Lives in a box under the toaster,
He's a very big brute and boaster,
Eats lots and lots of washing,
Comes out at night, sloshing and boshing,
In a big pile of pants and socks,
His name rocks and it is Dave,
No one knows why his mother gave him that name,
I suppose that is the only one she knew,
Because his great, great, great grandfather was called Dave too,
His eyes are black and his tongue is blue,
He looks like he has gone down the loo,
When the washing monster tries to speak,
It comes out, "Gobblee gabally geek!"
And when wash time comes,
Dave thinks, *this bobbady bums*,
I'm just joking, you silly scums,
When night-time comes, the washing monster says, "Goodbye."

Freya Baker (10)

Our Lady Of Mount Carmel Catholic Primary School, Tout Hill

Very Burnt Breakfast

V ery hot breakfast on the sun
E veryone is having fun
R ed-hot egg white
Y ellow yolk glooping around

B lack edge all around
U nder the sun, the hens lay eggs
R ound and round you go
N orth is not where you go, no no, not on
T he sun

B reakfast is the most important meal of the day
R ed-hot burning eggs, they need to pay
E ggs, eggs, eggs
A *rgh!* Hot, hot, hot
K ick the burnt one away
F aster eggs, hurry up
A s fast as you can!
S *izzle, sizzle*
T he eggs are done, yum yum!

Amelia Enticott (10)
Our Lady Of Mount Carmel Catholic Primary School, Tout Hill

Underneath The Reef

Underneath the reef
Lay creatures up to mischief
Jellyfish and sharks
Were being cheeky underneath the park.

They were having a party
Playing and darting
Jellyfish squirming
Sharks were lurking.

They were not the usual type
There were lots of magical music pipes!
Sails drifted, thinking, *what?*
Something's really heavy and fat!

There was singing.
I'd never heard a shark sing
Let alone a pair of two
It was loud
I didn't know what to do!
Jellyfish dancing, sharks cruising.

It went on 24/7
Louder and louder until it hurt!
It went even louder, not the worst
Sharks, fish, even people joined in
It was definitely a win-win!

Jasmine Palmer (10)

Our Lady Of Mount Carmel Catholic Primary School, Tout
Hill

Devil Doughnut

Once on a pizza planet,
There was a devil doughnut.
He was not a kind king.
Devil Doughnut took Ticklish Tomato,
Off the throne!

Creative Cookie went to war,
With Devil Doughnut.
And Devil Doughnut won the weird war (sadly).
Pizza Planet got half-eaten by Devil Doughnut,
And a talking pickle ate the rest!

Devil Doughnut, Ticklish Tomato and all the other
food,
Went to excellent Earth,
And sneakily saw the pickle.
Devil Doughnut took over Earth,
And mysteriously magicked all the food to talk!

Devil Doughnut got eaten,
By Pondering Pickle,
And I ate...
All the rest!

Hannah Power (10)

Our Lady Of Mount Carmel Catholic Primary School, Tout
Hill

The Best Friends

There once was a blueberry,
who liked to have a party,
at his auntie's.
To the party, a pineapple came,
the blueberry took a picture,
and put it in a frame.
They had a biscuit,
and decided to whisk it,
and fed it to the cat.
Then the blueberry put on a hat.
Blueberry had a thought,
whilst knocking on a door,
he wanted to make a biscuit Earth,
but the only gun he had was a Nerf.
He went to the kitchen,
while the cat was itching.
Pineapple came,
they played games,
all night and all day,
the best friends played.

James Adams (10)
Our Lady Of Mount Carmel Catholic Primary School, Tout
Hill

Halloween Treats Termination

When autumn comes, the leaves will crunch,
On Halloween, you get to munch,
The leaves now orange, no longer green,
Lots of ghosts are usually seen.

Zombies always arise,
At midnight,
The birds will flee,
We don't see what they see.

Pumpkins roar fire,
Henchmen they'll hire,
They'll steal sweets,
No more treats.

Children will disappear,
That's when evil's near,
Lighting up fires,
Survivors are liars.

This is what happens on Halloween night,
Is this the night you'll have a fright?

Roxanne Wylie (10)
Our Lady Of Mount Carmel Catholic Primary School, Tout Hill

The Talking Pickle!

The pickle had a giggle,
when the person did a tickle,
he was green and loved plants,
he also held a lot of ants,
in his tiny little hands.
He went to war,
to eat a door,
he left to eat a pizza planet,
and he came back with a bit of an ache in his
stomach.
So he went to the gym,
and lost a limb,
and couldn't get off the floor.
So he went home to fix himself,
and failed miserably.
He heard a loud noise and,
fell down to his little toes.
Turned out the pickle needed some rest,
before he could do his best.

Zuzanna Jaroni (10)
Our Lady Of Mount Carmel Catholic Primary School, Tout
Hill

Mrs Unorganised

Mrs Unorganised would like to go climbing,
but she can't get things quite right with her timing.
Her house is a very big mess,
and she will get into a big stress,
she also wears a dirty dress.
She has paperwork everywhere!
And even has a mess in her hair.
She never lets her friends come round,
from her, they never hear a sound.
As you can see, she can't get things right,
which is why she's awake all night.
You can see there are things she can never find,
but you'll have to wait 'til next time.

Ola Kopyto (10)
Our Lady Of Mount Carmel Catholic Primary School, Tout
Hill

The Runner

Run away before they come,
or you will become one of them,
run to the city so you are safe.

Infected monstrosities roam all around,
your world is in peril, so run to the safe place,
the infected are coming, so turn away.

Hooray! We've found a cure,
I hear something under the floor,
let's go and see what it is,
I'll open the door and... what is this?

An infected colony!
Quick, quick, give them the cure!
Munch, munch...

Maxine Lampard (10)
Our Lady Of Mount Carmel Catholic Primary School, Tout
Hill

Super Dog

Once I saw a dog,
He was a super dog,
He could walk, talk or fly to the moon,
But he just had to have a serious groom.

He caught many baddies,
For example, Devil Doughnut,
He never knew,
What was coming next,
But he definitely knew,
Who was the best.

He had laser eyes,
And a bone-flavoured gun,
To shoot the criminals' big fat bums.
Once he got,
An amazing red cape.
That's how Super Dog,
Got his namesake.

Nadia Bohdan (9)
Our Lady Of Mount Carmel Catholic Primary School, Tout
Hill

Super Potato

Super Potato is a kind, fun potato,
he will fight crime forever,
as long as he gets up after hours,
to see another parking fine,
he loves to call Mr Power,
to hear a ladybird sing,
it sounds like a ring,
hour after hour, he is singing all night,
after the crime is done, he watches 'Crazy Custard',
Super Potato is always singing,
too much, it sends you flying,
he's loved his mum since he was a little potato,
and she finds it funny.

Lewis Williams (10)
Our Lady Of Mount Carmel Catholic Primary School, Tout
Hill

Bon Bons

The Bon Bons loved adventures
They loved being adventurous
They walked through war
And booked a tour

They had a party
And went to their auntie
They played on the trampoline
And loved to play the tambourine

But one day they got put
In a packet
And one said, "Let's whack it!"
So they all started whacking

They came free
And found a bee
Which led them back home.

Bethany Barnett (10)
Our Lady Of Mount Carmel Catholic Primary School, Tout
Hill

Bendy And The Ink Machine

In this dark, inky, horrifying room
One mammal is waiting for you
Don't stop!
Keep on running through the night.

Find a way to keep your life.
Fear the mammal.
Flee the mammal.
Keep on running through the night.

Death is waiting in the room.
If you stay, it will come for you
The ink machine needs your blood to work
Keep on running through the night, Bendy.

Daniel David Colohan (9)

Our Lady Of Mount Carmel Catholic Primary School, Tout
Hill

George's Medicine

Sat by my cauldron
I have my grandpa
All his human medicine is gone
So I have to give him a great big shock
Not the kind that will see him go bang like a
balloon!
I need to mix a magical woohoo potion
That will clean up his insides.
It will fizzle and sizzle
Better watch out, Grandpa
Or I might accidentally turn you into a frog.

Edward Cutts (9)

Our Lady Of Mount Carmel Catholic Primary School, Tout
Hill

Swimming With Snakes And Snapping Turtles

At my house, there are
slithery, slimy snakes
and a big, fat, snapping turtle.
His name is Mertle
he is a chomper
he munches bumpers one after the other.
The reptiles hiss and they hiss
what do they wish?
Hissing at people
but
they always miss.
They love to swim
they are too fast
they love a blast.

Zachary Palmer (9)

Our Lady Of Mount Carmel Catholic Primary School, Tout Hill

Foxy Woxy

Riding on a six-legged milk and cookie fox,
Right next to a milk and cookie ox.
The fox doesn't like to eat,
But the ox likes to eat meat.
I like my music loud,
I like to look at my favourite cloud.
There is a big crash,
It makes a big smash.
It's been a nice ride,
Now we're starting to fry.

Tomas Sims (10)
Our Lady Of Mount Carmel Catholic Primary School, Tout
Hill

Riding On A Bird

A bird wearing golden glasses is riding through a cloud of jelly,
carrying a big fat belly,
he is very smelly,
wearing muddy wellies.

A bird is flying through the air,
with a speedy pace, soaring past the sun.
Remembering his flight over puddles, seeing a lost football,
on his way to see his mum.

Joshua Ruppersbery (9)
Our Lady Of Mount Carmel Catholic Primary School, Tout Hill

Is Peppa Bacon Or Not?

Are all pigs going to be bacon?
Eating lots of bacon...
Yum, yum, yum.

Are Peppa and George living bacon?
Will they become cartoon bacon?
Yuck, yuck, yuck.

I love real bacon and sausages.
But I wouldn't eat Peppa and George!
Let them keep jumping in muddy puddles!

Olivier Piatek (10)

Our Lady Of Mount Carmel Catholic Primary School, Tout
Hill

Donkey Monkey

In the forest lived a monkey
The monkey was called Donkey
In the desert there was a house of crisps
The person in that house was called Chris

In the desert lived a cactus
The cactus was called Pac-Man
The desert was very hot
And it felt like a frying pan.

Sergio Manuel Maleiro (10)

Our Lady Of Mount Carmel Catholic Primary School, Tout
Hill

Llama In My Bed

I found a llama in my bed,
Llama drama was over my head,
The llama went and said,
"I'm going to bed because of my head."
I said, "Go to sleep, Drama Llama,
Don't go to my neighbour's, 'cause it will alarm
'er."

Katie Berry (9)

Our Lady Of Mount Carmel Catholic Primary School, Tout
Hill

Surfing On A Cloud

I'm in the skies in Alaska,
surfing with a bowl of pasta,
seeing the land from up very high,
my dessert is a strawberry pie,
on the horizon, Anchorage lies.

Filip Wasyleczko (9)
Our Lady Of Mount Carmel Catholic Primary School, Tout
Hill

My Dog Spoke To Me

It'd been a long day in school, so I rushed home,
And when I got there, my dog was talking on my phone!
I took it away and shouted, "You naughty dog!"
But soon, he began to croak like a frog!
I heard this and said, "What's wrong with you?"
That's when he began to speak to me too.

I rushed him into the car, no time to lose,
With nothing on my feet because he'd eaten my shoes!
We arrived at the vet and I said to the nurse,
"My dog, my dog! It's like he's got a curse!"
She took him into the room and then explained,
"You really think I'll fall for this game?"
I glanced at her, she thought I was lame,
But then my dog was barking again!

Caitlin Price (10)

Somerset Bridge Primary School, Bridgwater

My Frustrating Poem!

I am going to enter the Poetry Wonderland
competition,
But school gets in the way (even in maths with my
addition),
My head is going off like a bomb,
In my poem, so many things could go wrong,
At night in my bed,
I think about winning in my head,
I know I might not have a chance,
Maybe I could write about horses who dance?
I don't know what to do! This is the thing,
What about a bell that always goes *ping?*
The next day, I have help from my friend,
I know it is cheating and breaking the rules, which
is a bend,
I hope they don't find out!
Because rumours could spread about!
From this day, I won!
In it, there's a bit of a pun,
If you're writing a poem, it will be okay,
If you win, it will be your day!

Don't stress!
Or your poem may be a mess!

Maizie-May Conway (10)

Somerset Bridge Primary School, Bridgwater

The Lost Hybrid Princess

Where are we?
What is wrong with me?
We're in a forest, don't you see?
Nothing much but you and me.

We're lost - we don't know where to go,
oh, but I think I hear a tree,
or a foot,
in a boot.
Nothing but us though.

I hear you flapping around up in the sky,
but now it's time to go up high,
to see where we are,
but my outfit will tear,
but I don't care anymore,
because we need to get home before we are
caught.

We're halfway there,
wind in my hair,
my little dragon all puffed up,
flying for too long in the air.

Home at last,
my little dragon, we're home at last!
We both dance and dance the night away,
until the dawn of the next day.

Ruby Elizabeth Boobyer (10)
Somerset Bridge Primary School, Bridgwater

I Sewed The Scales To A Mermaid's Tail!

I was swimming in the sea
When a shark came and brought some scales for
the mermaid to swim free
I was sewing the scales onto the mermaid's tail
and I sewed her tail all up
and then she began to swim
she said, "My tail is back to normal!
Thanks to the shark
for getting the scales for me!"
She requested for me
to see her family
in a dark, beautiful cave
it was covered in jewels
and there was a chest filled with diamonds
for us to take home.
I offered the shark a plate of chicken curry
for his help
but none would pass his lips
as he said, "I'm a vegetarian."

Sadie McSweeney-Stevens (10)
Somerset Bridge Primary School, Bridgwater

Sunbathe On A Cloud

My sunbathe on a cloud did not go to plan,
As I tumbled down and down,
I passed through other clouds and got so soaked,
A bird is what I landed on,
It suddenly threw me off,
And I landed on a plane,
Only to be windscreen wipered off!
It was very disappointing,
Being flipped off a bird,
Then I remembered, remembered, remembered,
The chute on my back,
And to pull the deployer,
But there were holes in the parachute,
That came from a hedgehog who was also diving down,
There I was, non-stop falling,
Only to land on a trampoline and front flip off,
To go about my daily routine.

Flynn Stuckey (10)
Somerset Bridge Primary School, Bridgwater

Surf On An Erupting Volcano

I surfed on the erupting volcano's lava
I could feel the heat in my toes
I heard the bubbling lava rising
Then ITV News came down the volcano
Someone else was having a barbecue
The wind blew and a sausage flew
It landed in my mouth
I ate it and it was delicious
I licked my fingers after eating my sausage
A Nutella jar came with a spoon
Luckily, I caught it in my hands
I said, "Time to eat something else!"
Of course, I ate it all up
Suddenly, money flew at me
I said, "Money, money, money!"
Then the lava shot straight up as I finished my surf.

Gracjan Kapral (10)

Somerset Bridge Primary School, Bridgwater

86

An Underwater Olympics

Having an Olympics under the sea,
is quite a silly idea, so now listen to me,
and here are the reasons why...

Trying to do the shot-put,
when there comes an octopus,
which sucks it from your hand.
Trying to do the high jump,
when all your diving gear weighs you down.
Trying to do the pole vault,
when an eel's nibbling at the pole.
Trying to do the races,
we'll have a winner soon,
when a great white is on your tail.

See, such a ridiculous idea!
Having an Olympics under the sea,
is a silly idea, so now listen to me.

Jack Turner (10)
Somerset Bridge Primary School, Bridgwater

Midnight Monster

I opened the door to find
A monster that was kind
It was very late at night
Oh, it gave me such a fright

It grabbed my hand so tight
Then we set off on a flight
We headed to the moon
Then Jupiter exploded with a boom!

A shooting star came rushing by
With all our might, we jumped up high
Then it brought us close to land
And dropped us on a marching band

The sun was rising now
There was mooing from the cows
I started heading home
Then I gave him a bone
I saw him fade away
What a spectacular day!

Casey Pester (10)
Somerset Bridge Primary School, Bridgwater

I Invited An Elf To Tea

I invited an elf to tea because I
felt I could see kindness in him
for never did I feel
this would be a big deal

But... he crushed my china plate
making him seem
very clearly mean
charging in my house
nothing like a mouse

Disobeying rules
making us seem like fools
up and down the stairs
round and round the bends
I warn you to never...
I warn you not to ever...
invite an elf to tea!
For he has no manners
for the elf I hope you see
is one of the most dreadful creatures to please.

Mia Charlotte Hawkins (10)
Somerset Bridge Primary School, Bridgwater

Jump On A Cactus

Jumping on a cactus is really quite mad
But up in the air, you don't feel sad
Messing around on pointy prickles
Would probably be like pins and needles.

Onto the spikes that hurt your bottom
Because they can get through thick cotton.

A cactus is so much more than just a green thing
Standing up tall.

Calling out when you've got one stuck
Amazing how cool a cactus is
They have more defences than humans.

Jumping on a cactus is really quite mad
But up in the air, you don't feel sad.

Sophia Heal (10)
Somerset Bridge Primary School, Bridgwater

Bubble Mania

I spilt my bubbles,
and out came a couple,
of bubble dogs.

Exploring around,
then out came a sound,
a squeak from a bubble dog.

I fed them some blueberries,
to find a surprise - they were turning blue!
I fed them some strawberries,
to yet again find,
that they were turning red.

I spotted that one of them was falling asleep,
as the other one took a leap,
it landed on my lap as fast as I could clap,
"Night night, little bubble dogs!" I said.

Tilly Stevens (10)
Somerset Bridge Primary School, Bridgwater

A Wish Come True

One day, I picked up a dandelion,
Wished for happiness,
And blew the fairies away.
Off they went,
Floating elegantly,
To complete their mission.

Days later, they came back,
Flying with a present on their lap.
They handed it over,
And flew away.

The present was small indeed,
It was ten times smaller than me!
I watched them peacefully rest on the ground,
And I opened my gift.

It came out with swirls and magic,
I think it was a wish come true.

Jessica Knight (11)
Somerset Bridge Primary School, Bridgwater

My Pet Elephant

I was in Australia,
when I found my first pet,
I then met a vet,
he said he was in need,
I then went to buy a lead.

I got on a plane,
it flew down,
so I held it tight,
so it didn't give me a fright.

I made it home,
my mum was proud,
I found an ice cream cone,
I wrapped it in a tissue.

I gave it to the elephant,
it picked up the phone,
it then turned pink and flew away with my hat,
the next day,
it dropped on the doormat.

Lilly-Ann Weaver (10)
Somerset Bridge Primary School, Bridgwater

Flying A Spitfire

Flying a Spitfire through the air,
looking down at the nodding grass below,
passing Hurricanes and flying dogs,
looking up at the fluffy candyfloss in the sky.

Flying a Spitfire through the wind,
shooting the cannons at the squabbling
Messerschmitts.

Flying up and down,
side to side,
ever thinking about when the fight will end.

Flying a Spitfire down to the ground,
landing at an airfield at the end of the flight,
getting put away for the next night.

Toby Larwood (10)
Somerset Bridge Primary School, Bridgwater

My Food Travels

I jump onto my banana rocket,
Off I go,
High I fly,
In the sky.

I'm here,
Crisp planes flying overhead,
Wonder where they're going?

There it is,
Pizza Palace,
Owned by King Ketchup.

Lolly fences,
Oh-so sweet,
Can I have a nice treat to eat?

Off to Planet Burger where I stay,
Take out my mushroom make-up brushes,
I dive into the cheese where the fire is lit,
Playing cookie cards with my friends.

Lorelei Murdoch (10)
Somerset Bridge Primary School, Bridgwater

Under The Sea

Under the sea
Is where I want to be

I don't like land
But I do like smooth sand

Sand massages my feet
For me, it's a big treat

A dazzling seahorse
Was on an underwater racecourse

There I saw a squid
That was very well hid

There was a wrecked pirate ship
Where a whale had a little kip

I love the cold sea
But after, I have a warm cup of tea
But it's all squidtastic.

Aaron Bojko (10)
Somerset Bridge Primary School, Bridgwater

That Day Of '87

One day, me and my two friends
Evie and the crying child
went to Fazbear Pizzeria.
Let me tell you about them.
Evie was really fun, funny and loopy.
The crying child believed in spirits
I did too
but there was something weird about his Fredbear
plush toy.
Whenever I saw it, it was talking.
The crying child's brother, Terrance,
was very mean.
Shortly after, the spring lock failed
I noticed that I was now magical...

Grace Payne (10)
Somerset Bridge Primary School, Bridgwater

Have A Genie As A Pet

It's a bad idea, having a genie as a pet,
Because the only thing he does is what he wants,
He won't listen to what I say,
I don't know what to do,
That's the thing,
It's the only hope,
My genie is just so bad,
The way I feel about my genie is: he makes me sad,
My genie sometimes gets lost,
My genie even makes a mess,
My genie even breaks my sister's toys,
I need another genie to get rid of him.

Cynthia Sosnowska (10)

Somerset Bridge Primary School, Bridgwater

Tea Party With A Troll

Once I invited a troll for tea
He smiled with glee
And said, "Sure, I'll come for tea!"
As we started eating
I realised I'd made a mistake
I could barely swallow my steak!
He gobbled down his jam tart
Licking his fingers after
Something happened next
I didn't expect
He picked his nose!
That sent shivers down my spine
Then he flung it on the wall
That was it
I sent him home!

Libby Coupland (11)
Somerset Bridge Primary School, Bridgwater

Greedy Jay

Far, far away, a boy called Jay ran to ruin my day
First, he took my pants and socks
So I couldn't get changed for seven o'clock
Secondly, I went downstairs to see what I'd got
But when I looked in the fridge to see what I'd got
I realised that I'd lost the lot
Because greedy Jay had got there first!
The next day, I was fed and ready for work
And all was fine, but the time was nine!

Charlie Coles (10)
Somerset Bridge Primary School, Bridgwater

My Cloud Adventure

On a cloud I lay,
Moonbathing all day,
Off I fell,
I landed in pain.

I found myself on a roller coaster,
Off it went,
I landed,
Oh!

Cotton candy trees,
A Nutella river,
Animals all mixed,
Elephants with long necks and pig noses.

Flying monkeys,
Zebras with manes,
Rabbits with horns,
And giraffes with trunks.

Jenna Frances Lyddon-Roberts (10)
Somerset Bridge Primary School, Bridgwater

I Saw

I saw a sheep
It leapt into the deep.

I saw a turtle
Jumping a hurdle.

I saw a pig
Eating a fig.

I saw a lion
It was lying, obviously.

I saw a cat
Wearing a fancy hat.

I saw a horse
It was on a racecourse.

These wacky creatures
Don't like their features
But I think they are amazing!

Kieran Upham (11)

Somerset Bridge Primary School, Bridgwater

Panda Time

P layful times at the zoo
A lways there, looking for you!
N aughty pandas hide away too
D elicious bamboo they eat for food
A panda has a playful mood!

T oday was a great day
I would never like to go away!
M aybe there is a way I could stay
E ven if I was a zookeeper, hip hip hooray!

Naomi Wiacek (10)

Somerset Bridge Primary School, Bridgwater

The Crazy Artist

There was once a crazy artist who lived next door
He'd draw and draw his dog called Paws.
Excited and amazed
Paws gazed into space.
As the artist bent down to tie up his lace
He knocked down a glass of chalk
Later that day, he went on a walk
To paint his favourite bug
A slug!
Of course!

Millie Doughty (11)
Somerset Bridge Primary School, Bridgwater

Candy Land

Have you ever been to Candy Land?
It has chocolate, truffles and coconuts - it's really grand
Gummy bears, even a gumball ever so bright
White chocolate seagulls fly like kites

Gummy bears drinking Coke from bottles that explode
Strawberry and lime snakes slithering across the road
Chocolate Flake soil where the gummy worms live
Liquorice and Haribo trees, oh so massive!

Candy Land had its own candy king
Who had a crown, cape and a golden ring
The king was bossy, greedy and fat
And strangely his pets were a cat and a bat!

One day, he was out for a walk in the park
But then he got lost and it began to get dark
He sat down to drink a milkshake from a cup
And a sweet-toothed dog came and gobbled him up!

Daniel Linsdell (8)
St Michael's Academy, Yeovil

Halo The Dinosaur

I'm a T-rex, I'm big and mean
I'm the biggest baddest dinosaur on the scene.

With my razor-sharp teeth
All shiny and clean.

I'm a T-rex, I'm big and mean,
I'm the biggest baddest dinosaur on the scene.

When people see me coming
They run and scream.

I'm a T-rex, I'm big and mean
Roar!

Troy Ford (7)
St Michael's Academy, Yeovil

Sweet, Sweet Jungle

The jelly toad hiding in the chocolate cake tree.
The toffee lion climbing over the toffee bridge.
The blueberry bubblegum river being swallowed by
the gummy lizard.
The chocolate monkey swinging on the strawberry
lace vine.
The rainbow parrot gazing at the Chocolate
Orange sun.
The explorer coming to eat it all up.

Lucas Conway (7)
St Michael's Academy, Yeovil

Milky Way

I went to the moon to buy some cheese,
But all that was there was rocks for me,
I was devastated for I'd flown all that way,
And I was stuck in the Milky Way.

Suddenly, I saw my sister flying away,
Up and over the galaxy,
I jumped into my rocket,
And chased her far away,
But then a big rock went in front of me,
So I dodged it but lost my way,
So I travelled back to the Milky Way.

Then I got my binoculars out to have a look,
And found my sister with a book,
She waved at me surprisingly,
Then we took hands,
And lived in the Milky Way,
Eating chocolate stars for eternity.

Sophie Webb (9)
St Philip's CE Primary School, Odd Down

Seawater Circus

I want to tell you a poem, it is all about me...
Full of joy with the fishes and dolphins diving in
and out of the sea.

This happened in the ocean and
my mum said it was bad to go out with a dolphin
for tea...

I had always imagined swimming in the ocean with
all of the fish.
Every time I went to the seaside, I tried to find fish,
It would be odd if the ocean had a road and fish
cars,
But there were just a lot of jellyfish.

I thought for a moment, *I'll go deep in the sea*,
I found a circus deep under the sea,
With turtles and dolphins and fish swimming free.
We had fun at the circus, my family and me,
Watching all of the creatures under the sea.

Cara Willcox (7)
St Philip's CE Primary School, Odd Down

A Dream Land Adventure

I fall asleep
An exciting moment I can't wait to meet
I see a teleporter and jump inside
With lots of excitement and filled with surprise
I shoot down a tube with lots of pace
This really feels like the fastest race
Like a lightning bolt with a jolt
I land in a world full of magic
I can see men dressed as ladies which looks rather tragic
I look up and see that it's raining hard
When I look closer, it's raining lumps of lard!
So I jump back into the teleporter
This weather is rather fraught
I'm now travelling to other lands without the risk of rain
Let's not go to a land full of pain
With another jolt, I land on Jupiter which is named after the Roman god
It is there I meet an alien called Tod
He looks rather funny, a bit like my mummy
I bet I looked like that when I came out of her tummy

We shake hands but then the teleporter begins to tumble
I think it's time to get ready to rumble
I jump back inside
The next thing I know, I'm awake outside.

Ben McLaughlan (9)
St Philip's CE Primary School, Odd Down

I Live In Space

You may think that this is strange
But I really do live in space.
If you think I sound funny
I can even show you my space buddy.
I have seen cheese on the moon
However, I've only been there at noon.
But the most annoying thing about the moon
Is that there is nothing there to do.
I have a house made of a meteorite
So you might want to hold on tight!
There is life here but you just don't know it
There are fluffy, furry animals
And not any sort of aggressive cannibals.
There are a few picky beasts
But that is if you don't give them their treats.
Now your question might be:
What do I eat?
Now the thing is, the scientists down there are,
Not really honest for the planets are not
Made of gas but simply sweets and edible grass.
My most favourite thing that I like

Is that I got a free rocket
Without even needing to pay any money from my
own pocket.
So now you know what goes on up here
Tell your parents to listen carefully with their ears.

Nathan Saji John (10)

St Philip's CE Primary School, Odd Down

The Adventures Of Patch The Dog

Patch was a dog with a dream
A dream to travel the world
Then one day, his dream came true
And he packed his bags to go

Croatia was first on the list
He had some great fun on the plane
But felt weary when he arrived
So had a swim to wake himself up

He then had a Thai massage
And lay back to catch the rays
The next day, he climbed some rocks
And visited some of the sights

His trip was near its end
He watched the setting sun
The next day, he headed home
To the bed where he belonged
(Todd's bed).

Todd Clay (10)
St Philip's CE Primary School, Odd Down

There's A Giraffe In My Bath!

There's a giraffe in my bath
What am I going to do?
I need to get him out
Before he does a number two!
My mum won't be happy
If he poos in the bath
But if I'm really honest
I think I'd probably laugh!
I call the fire engine
And ask them for a ladder
"Please come quick, I'm laughing so hard
I'm worried about my bladder!"
So the firemen come and winch him out
Using a massive crane
"Thank goodness he's gone, there's no poo in my bath
And I can relax again!"

Gracie Williams (8)
St Philip's CE Primary School, Odd Down

High Up A Tree

One day, I climbed up a tree,
it was tall, about 100 times bigger than me,
and on that day, I went up and up,
but then I thought, *oh no, what if I get stuck?*
so on that note, I went down,
until I saw the bear waiting around for me to be found,
but very soon after I'd seen the bear,
I looked up at the tree and thought, *I'd be much better up there.*
so I sped up, going from branch to branch to get away,
but it took a while for me to accept that the distance was okay,
soon after, I found a comfy spot and I was still,
and I was only awake because I heard the roar of the bear before it made a kill,
so I climbed higher and higher and higher,
I finally realised that I'd reached the spire,
I stayed there for years and years,
all because of my mighty fears,
so if I were to give my advice to you,

here's what I think you should do,
if you want to climb a tree,
check for bears, don't be like me.

Jasper Richardson (11)

St Philip's CE Primary School, Odd Down

Wonderland Olympics

At the Wonderland Olympics, all the beasts took part.
The mermaids did the swimming and the goblins raced in a cart.

In the giant's basketball game, the hoops were in the clouds.
The roaring of the Minotaur was drowned out by the crowd.

The unicorns were doing dressage with rainbow ribbons in their hair.
The pixies were riding alicorns and flying in the air.

Pegasus did the hurdles, the centaurs fired their bows.
The dwarves threw their hammers and the winners sat in rows.

The queen gave out the medals and the dragons lit the flames.
The winners stood on toadstools at the ending of the games.

Lilly Dyer (9)
St Philip's CE Primary School, Odd Down

The Hungry Horse

The horse was standing in its field,
He was bored of grass and hay.
He thought it was a really good idea,
To eat at a restaurant that day.

He had to think where he could go,
Where would be a good place to eat.
He heard the farmer say that he liked,
The Hungry Horse for a real treat.

He left his field and went down the road,
He saw a building, "It must be here!"
He went and sat at a table,
And said, "Meatballs, chips and bacon,
And maybe beer."

Charlie Williams (8)
St Philip's CE Primary School, Odd Down

Candyland

I woke up in the morning and what did I see?
A cotton candy wonderland staring back at me.
There were trees with trunks of chocolate logs,
And leaves made of Freddo frogs.
The grass was red in several places,
And made of strawberry laces.
I jumped out of bed and got dressed in a hurry,
I rushed outside of my house to see if I could find a chocolate bunny.
I sat down on the strawberry grass and fed myself a handful,
There were flowerbeds of lollipops and all my favourite treats.
So I picked up another couple of handfuls and ate them very fast,
Scared that this magic wonderland might not last.
In no time at all, my belly was well fed,
Then I rolled over and realised I was still in bed.
It was all just a dream and not true at all,
But when I go to bed again, I hope I do return.

Tia Jovanovska (7)
St Philip's CE Primary School, Odd Down

My Crazy Family

My crazy family likes to go to the beach,
When we get in the sea, my sister goes mental and
I float around like a lentil!
My crazy family loves to go to the park,
Every time we go, my mum likes to swing all the
way round on the swings and ends up in a pile of
bins!
My crazy family loves to eat chocolate,
Our faces get all smeared and it looks like a beard!
My crazy family loves to cuddle,
When we do, we get in a big muddle!
My crazy family likes to play in the garden,
We have a trampoline and we jump like loons and
try and try to reach the moon!
My family may be crazy,
But I love them all the same, even though we are
all insane!

Charlie Pym (10)
St Philip's CE Primary School, Odd Down

Monsters Are Funny

Monsters are big, some are scary,
Some are little and some are fairies,
Monsters mini, monsters massive,
Monsters crawling under your bed,
Monsters playing in the hedge,
Monsters are hairy, monsters are messy,
Some monsters are kind, some monsters are mean,
Monsters like to eat green beans,
Monsters like to tell you jokes,
They sometimes crack egg yolks,
So when you hear a monster yell,
You'd better beware,
Because it might rip out your hair.

Samuel James Kindon (9)
St Philip's CE Primary School, Odd Down

A Turtle And A Dragon

Myrtle the turtle was swimming in the sea,
"I wonder when my babies will hatch and come
and join me?"
Dave the dragon was dreaming about his dinner,
"If I don't eat soon, I'll get thinner and thinner."
Night fell and all you could hear,
Was the sound of baby turtles heading for the pier,
All except Bob the tiny turtle who went towards
the road,
He couldn't hear the sea, only the croaking of a
toad.
Dave the dragon came and saved the day,
He lit 100 fires to show Bob the way to the bay.
Myrtle was so relieved that Bob had made it to the
water,
That she fainted, but Dave was there and caught
her.
To celebrate Bob's safety and Dave the amazing
beast,
Myrtle made her friend an enormous midnight
feast!

Robbie Skellern (10)

St Philip's CE Primary School, Odd Down

The Magical Creature Poem

Deep in the woods
Little creatures bring goods
A unicorn, a griffin and a dragon
They are magically wheeled out of a mini door on a wagon.

The griffin flaps out books with his wings
"Wow!" says the king
The unicorns poos words
Farts can be heard
The dragon breathes out pictures
Happy and confused are their feelings, a mixture.

They make golden, silver and bronze books,
Which have lots of cool looks.

Emmy Habgood (7)
St Philip's CE Primary School, Odd Down

The Sting Of The Jellyfish

The jellyfish stings me, I shout, "Ouch!"
At the bottom of my head and the tip of my snout,
It hurts! It hurts! I know, I know,
And the sting! The sting, it's starting to grow,
I know I need to calm myself down but, oh no!
The jellyfish is starting to frown,
The king of them all is charging at me,
But the size of him, wow! He's as tall as a tree,
I'm literally swimming as fast as I can,
But I wish I was as fast as the fastest man,
Someone please! Help me please!

Oliver Hutchings (9)

St Philip's CE Primary School, Odd Down

The Big Burger

I wake up and wonder
Why there is a burger
Right at the end of my bed.
It's bigger than me
And towers like a tree
Is there something wrong with my head?
I rub my eyes in disbelief
I think I am having a dream
This is the most gigantic burger I have ever seen!
I open my mouth to take a big bite
I can't resist the smell
But the burger has other plans - to eat *me* up...
This dream hasn't ended so well!

Harry Williams (10)
St Philip's CE Primary School, Odd Down

Yummy And Yucky Food

I love yummy cake with jam in the middle and a
cherry on top.
You can eat it as a snack.
You can eat it in a lunch box.
You can eat it any time.
I do not like slimy mushrooms, yucky!
My mum gives me slimy mushrooms in pasta,
It's like eating squishy slugs!
Grown-ups eat disgusting food,
Like soup, porridge, risotto and cabbage.
If I was a grown-up, I would eat,
Sweets, chocolate, doughnuts and jelly,
For breakfast, lunch and dinner!

Daisy Ann Gregory (7)
St Philip's CE Primary School, Odd Down

The Light Fury

In a land above the clouds, there are lots of
dragons free to fly wherever they want.
Change wings, screaming death, the fiery worm
queen, all protectors...
But there is one dragon who is the leader of all the
dragons.
The Light Fury!
Big and sparkly white, she is the queen of the skies!

Wherever she goes, she leaves a trail of snow,
shiny with ice.
In danger, she is as powerful as 100 warriors.
When she passes by, all the other dragons bow
down to her.
She is the queen of the skies!

Matthew Bradley (7)
St Philip's CE Primary School, Odd Down

Autumn Animals

Hedgehogs creep around at night,
Looking for a tasty bite,
Hoglets await their parent's return,
So they can eat their tasty worm.

The wise old owl sits up in his house,
Waiting to swoop down on the unsuspecting
mouse.

The sly old fox is looking for pickings,
When he stumbles across a hut full of chickens,

As the sun comes up for another day,
These three animals hide away.

Eleanor May Favager (10)
St Philip's CE Primary School, Odd Down

The Candy Planet

Do you have a secret place?
I can tell you that I do,
There is a land called Sweet Tooth Planet,
That I can travel to.

It can be our little secret,
But I really shouldn't talk,
I get there through a portal,
I drew it with magic chalk.

Sweet Tooth Planet is a place,
Where the white chocolate river flows,
Candyfloss hills with lollipop trees,
And it rains marshmallows.

The liquorice track is lots of fun,
And the gingerbread cats are great,
But playing in this magic place,
Is better with a mate.

So take this chalk away with you,
And a portal you should make,

Draw a circle and jump in,
Meet me at Gumdrop Lake.

Jayden Draper (9)
St Philip's CE Primary School, Odd Down

The Dangerous Dragon

The dangerous dragon lives in a cave
No one can challenge him except the brave
There was a young boy who walked for days
To find the dragon that lives in a cave

He crept on in to the mysterious place
Lurking in the dark was the dragon's face
With a step and a stumble, the little boy fell
Down, down, down into the well

He has not been seen again since that day
But still the dragon lies in that very cave.

Riley Prior (9)
St Philip's CE Primary School, Odd Down

The Time Dragon

T he ferocious dragon hunting its prey in the forest.

I n the forest, everything he breathes on goes back in time.

M oney forming on the ground as he breathes on it.

E verything getting changed by accident by the silly dragon.

D ead ends forming in front of the silly, peculiar dragon.

R omans getting up off the ground and attacking the dragon.

A nglo-Saxons running away from the exotic beast.

G iants attacking the dragon and Romans.

O n the dragon's back are dodo birds that are biting him.

N ewton rubbing his head where the apple hit his head (it was actually a stone thrown by one of the Anglo-Saxons).

Ethan O'Connor (10)

St Philip's CE Primary School, Odd Down

Owls Flying Past Bath (City)

Owls hoot, owls fly,
But these ones are going past Bath.
There are hundreds of owls like these ones,
3D, digital and cool owls,
Black see-through owls,
Sparkly short owls,
Gold gruff owls,
Snowy rainbow owls,
Glow-in-the-dark owls,
Flowery beautiful owls,
Sweet lovely owls,
Fleeing owls,
Black owls
And many, many more owls!

Reuben John Waldron (9)
St Philip's CE Primary School, Odd Down

The Spooks Of Halloween Special

When the ghosts scream and the children squirm,
You know Halloween's coming,
The pumpkins are bright in the dead of night,
The children scaring all,
Vampires and witches,
Cauldron fires bursting into flames,
Skeleton bones making children run home,
The werewolves howl,
And the monsters growl when the sun goes down,
When Halloween is done and the next day has begun,
We will not care for spooks and ghouls,
For we will be making our lists to Santa Claus.

Harry Houldsworth (10)
St Philip's CE Primary School, Odd Down

My Rubber Duck

My rubber duck
He is called Chuck
He is a happy little fellow
Who is very yellow

He has an orange beak
When you squeeze him, he goes *squeak!*
He floats in my bath
Like a little raft

When the bath comes to an end
I worry for my little friend
For out of the bath he goes
Onto the shelf, next to the toilet roll.

Corina Franklin (7)
St Philip's CE Primary School, Odd Down

The Magic Pigeon

Once a pigeon lived in a cave,
He did not know how to behave,
The pigeon was magic too,
He needed to know what to do,
He saw some sparks at the door,
And gave a big roar, roar, roar,
He went outside to explore,
Which he had never done before,
He suddenly was on an adventure,
In a cold December,
Following the sparks down the hill,
To where the dinosaur lived called Bill.

Bun Li (7)
St Philip's CE Primary School, Odd Down

While You Slept

As night closed in on the sleepy town,
And the large pale sun went slowly down.

Creatures rose up from the deep,
With gnarly toes and scaly feet,
They stalked around within the dark,
And crawled so quietly to the park.

They gobbled up the wooden benches,
And scoffed the bins with stinky stenches.

They chased each other to the store,
And battered down the old oak door,
They licked the children's favourite sweets,
And sniffed the fancy pastry treats.

But as the sun rose up again,
The monsters crawled back to their den,
Who they were we'll never know,
But out at night I'll never go.

Joel Atkinson (10)
St Philip's CE Primary School, Odd Down

Autumn

Autumn leaves, orange and brown
Swirling, dancing, covering the town
Falling gracefully as you sit by the fire
A warm hot chocolate is all you desire
The trees turn orange as leaves fall
The trees aren't very green at all
The brown conkers start to fall
From the golden trees that aren't very tall
The pretty flowers hide under the tree
Green, brown and orange leaves you can see
A cold, bitter breeze
Surrounds the autumn trees
Autumn winds begin to blow
Coloured leaves fall fast and slow
Leaves on the street
Leaves on my feet
Orange, yellow, red and green
Pretty like you've never seen.

Ava Parry-Smith (9)
St Philip's CE Primary School, Odd Down

Splish, Splash, Splish, Splash

As I jumped from lily pad to lily pad in a dash,
I could hear the water going *splish, splash, splish, splash!*
Under my feet, the lily pads wibbled and wobbled,
As I watched the fish blowing bubbles.

"Here fishy, fishy!" I said,
As I gently placed my finger in the water and tickled its scaly head,
Slowly, I could feel myself tipping into the warm water,
And suddenly, I saw a school of fish surrounding me with laughter.

Faith Adeline Baldeo (10)
St Philip's CE Primary School, Odd Down

Rugby

The grass is lush and green
I catch the ball and run like I have a rocket in my pocket
The wind blows through my hair as I run
I pass the ball behind me
I do a loop the loop back around to join the line
I get the ball back and run like I have a rocket in my pocket
The wind blows through my hair again
I score a try
I bounce as high as a kangaroo with joy
I love Saturdays cos rugby is my game.

Joshua Alan Scarrott (8)
St Philip's CE Primary School, Odd Down

Spiders

Spiders are really scary sometimes,
They make people jump sometimes,
People are usually scared of spiders when they see them.

Spiders can be black or grey,
But spiders don't usually prey,
They even spray.

They mostly make people scared,
Spiders are sometimes paired,
Sometimes they stare at each other.

Ivy Yang (8)
St Philip's CE Primary School, Odd Down

Sew These Scales To Me!

One day, I was walking along the beach,
When a beautiful mermaid from the sea called to me,
"Come sit down on this seaweed seat
And please sew these scales to my mermaid feet!"
Her call made me jump and I started to stare,
The sun glinted on her golden mermaid hair,
All of a sudden, a whale leapt high in the sky,
And the mermaid swam away in fright calling to me, "Bye-bye!"

Eryn Higgins (10)
St Philip's CE Primary School, Odd Down

Autumn

When summer goes and the temperature drops,
the leaves on the trees fall to the ground.
The squirrels are busy searching for nuts,
to store away in their winter huts.
The birds are busy making their nests,
from the leaves on the ground, they only pick the best.
Hedgehogs start gathering slugs and snails for their nests,
where they raise their hoglets and enjoy a nice rest.
The bunnies are running, playing hide-and-seek,
whilst the humans creep up and take a peek.
People are rushing to and fro,
to get their warmer clothes ready to go.

Ruby Grace Favager (8)
St Philip's CE Primary School, Odd Down

I Am A Gamer

I am a gamer,
I've been playing as long as I can remember,
I started on the PlayStation,
But I had a brief spell on the Xbox One,
Now back on the PlayStation,
I give it all my attention,
When I play a game called Fortnite,
I stay up and play all night,
And when I play, I'm like a boss,
Then I start to do the floss.

Oliver James Holt (10)
St Philip's CE Primary School, Odd Down

Popstar Poem

I've arrived in my purple Lamborghini,
I walk around nervously,
I'm in China, in a big fat place,
In front of 100,000 people,
I'm wearing a crop top and jeans,
With my microphone, mascara and purple-blushed
cheeks,
There are two, four, six, eight people in my group
of friends,
Five, four, three, two, one, onstage I go,
Screaaam!

Libby Mason (8)
St Philip's CE Primary School, Odd Down

Sweet Treats

I like eating chocolate bars of different shapes and sizes,

or perhaps a pot of jelly beans in all those crazy colours,

It's nice to have some popcorn on Fridays after school,

and to follow it with mint choc chip with sprinkles and sauce,

Who wants to have sprouts when cookies are around?

You have your five a day with some juicy Jelly Babies,

or satisfy your thirst with a cherry-flavoured coke!

Feel the burst of peppermint exploding in your mouth,

whilst munching chocolate buttons twenty at a time!

Anybody fancy a sweet treat?

Harry Hall (11)

St Philip's CE Primary School, Odd Down

Swimming

I like swimming because I like floating in the pool
I also like to sink, I think that's really cool!
I like front crawl because I like to wave my arms
My teacher is called Ollie, he is full of charm
I like blowing bubbles with my nose
And squirting water out of toys like a hose!
I like to do races and go really fast
But I don't like coming last
Diving is fun, I don't want to stop
Until I do a big belly flop!
When swimming is over, I don't like getting dressed after
It always ends up in a big disaster!

Chloe Pym (8)
St Philip's CE Primary School, Odd Down

Captain Jelly

Captain Jelly
Wears bright green wellies
He is a sight to see
As he wibble wobbles through the air
Without a care or any hair
He's the flavour of lime
But he still fights crime
He's brave and funny
All of the time
He's Captain Jelly
Don't be afraid.

Ryan Fender (7)
St Philip's CE Primary School, Odd Down

Books

Books have pages,
Suitable for all ages.
They have some themes,
And some pictures,
You can get them,
In different mixtures.
In a series,
You might see,
That they're similar,
To the one recently.
Books are funny,
Books are sad,
They might make you,
Very mad.
Short books,
Long books,
Thin books,
And thick books.
Fiction books are cool,
Non-fiction can be fun,

But only if it is about,
Football records that have been won.

Oscar Costello (10)
St Philip's CE Primary School, Odd Down

The Big Tree

I am climbing up a tree,
There's a monkey beside me,
Birds are flying up ahead,
I am starting to fill with dread,
The clouds are all below me,
Yet I climb higher and higher,
And there's a dragon breathing out fire!
I close my eyes and count to three,
I wake up and it's all a dream!

Shay Lewis (9)
St Philip's CE Primary School, Odd Down

Gymnastics

B askervilles is a gym in Bath.
A t the gym, we do fun activities.
S tar jumps on the trampoline.
K icking in the air.
E lephant walking all the time.
R unning very fast for the warm up.
V ault on, cartwheel off.
I go to the gym on Mondays.
L istening to coaches is what I do best.
L aughing all the time.
E nergy is all you need to be a gymnast like me.
S miling is what gymnastics makes me do every day!

Amelia May Hargreaves (8)

St Philip's CE Primary School, Odd Down

Secret Tunnel

S *hh!* It's a secret.

E *ek!* Bats are squeaking.

C *rumble!* Stones are falling!

R *umble!* The floor is vibrating!

E verything is wobbling!

T hen it stops vibrating.

T *umble!* The walls are shaking.

U nderground tunnels are the best.

N ote to self, don't come here again.

N othing, no sound at all.

E verything is quiet.

L ight, daylight.

Ezra Banham (9)

St Philip's CE Primary School, Odd Down

Dragon Mania

Some people think that dragons are not good,
But they helped the men as much as they could,
They breathe out fire,
And make the flames go higher,
It gives people a fright,
But it also gives them light,
When the dragons sleep, you'd better tiptoe
around them or,
They might wake up and eat you for dinner.

Elijah Baggan (7)

St Philip's CE Primary School, Odd Down

I Love Sports

My name is Corey and I like playing sports,
Any sport I can play, I will try any sort.

I have been swimming for the longest,
And I feel this is what makes me the strongest.

I enjoy playing cricket,
Bowling out opponents to take the wicket.

I play football in a team called the Pumas,
I train and practise with the others.

As I get older and stronger, I would like to try new things,
I hope by then, the Pumas will win and be as strong as kings.

Corey Summers (9)
St Philip's CE Primary School, Odd Down

Land Of Unicorns

Come to the land of unicorns where everything is different.
The smell of sweets will meet you with soft gentle music playing.
Where houses are made of candy.
Look up to the roofs made of chocolate buttons.
Walk up the Love Heart path.
Look through the lollipop windows to see the soft mallow furniture.
Why not knock on the door to see who might greet you?
Follow the rainbow lights to the magical waterfall.
There you'll meet the unicorns having a unicorn ball.

Sophie Mitchell (8)
St Philip's CE Primary School, Odd Down

The Odyssey Cross-Stitch

O dysseus is the hero in this Greek myth

D aringly, Odysseus ventured to the Land of the Dead

Y earning for home, Odysseus set sail from Ithaca

S adly, the Trojan War lasted for eleven years and still had no outcome

S urprisingly, the city of Troy was overcome by the Greeks

E nding the Trojan War, the Greeks built a wooden horse and filled it with men

Y ears went by, but Odysseus and his men still weren't home in Ithaca.

Willis Skardon (10)
St Philip's CE Primary School, Odd Down

The Bear In The Library

I stepped into the library, no one was there,
Except for a little baby bear,
I took some books, one or two,
One about bears and one about the moon,
I wondered if the baby had a mother,
Suddenly I heard breathing noises, one after another,
I saw the mother bear, I was about to shout,
But I was hiding behind a desk and quickly got out.

Maya Nascimento (10)
St Philip's CE Primary School, Odd Down

My Dog And Me

My dog is called Bramley and he's completely
crazy.
He's fun and playful and definitely not lazy.
He barks at conkers, he's totally bonkers!
He loves to chew, usually my shoe!
He's very quick and he loves to chase a stick.
My favourite time of all is when he's in the bath.
He shimmies and shakes and makes us all laugh.
Then he's clean, soft and loves a cuddle.
That is until he finds a puddle!
Uh-oh!

Ruby Treweek (8)
St Philip's CE Primary School, Odd Down

Autumn

A utumn leaves falling everywhere
U nderground, small mammals hibernating here and there
T he autumn colours - red, yellow and orange
U mbrellas found and dusted off for the rain
M igrating birds flying high in the sky
N ovember nights, cold and dark

F ires and fireworks warm the heart
U p they go, loud and bright
N ext comes winter and the frost, crispy and light.

Connor Snelling (10)
St Philip's CE Primary School, Odd Down

My Brother Who Thinks He's A Superhero

My little brother who is only three,
Thinks he's a superhero who can climb our garden tree,
"Not a good idea!" my little brother was told,
"You're far too small and not very old."
But do not fear my little brother, one day you will grow tall,
Our garden tree will then seem very small.

Cheyenne Moyle (9)
St Philip's CE Primary School, Odd Down

The Happy Asleep Cat

Whose cat is that? I think I know,
Its owner is quite happy though,
Full of joy like a beautiful rainbow,
I watch him play, I cry, "Hello!"
The cat is happy deep asleep,
But he has promises to keep,
After a feed and lots of sleep,
Sweet dreams come to him cheap,
He rises from his gentle bed,
With thoughts of kittens in his head,
He licks the butter off the bread,
Ready for the day ahead.

Morgan Currie (8)
St Philip's CE Primary School, Odd Down

If Pigs Could Fly

In the morning, I started yawning as I got out of
bed.
I opened the door and fell to the floor and badly
hurt my head.
I jumped off the floor and there I saw a pig fly by.
I rubbed my eyes and, to my surprise, there was a
pig casually in the sky.
In the sky so very high, no laws did apply, it was
just a pig that could fly.

Luke Thompson (10)

St Philip's CE Primary School, Odd Down

Crazy Slime

C razy slime is amazing.

R ats are in the slime.

A pples are in the slime.

Z oo animals are in the slime.

Y ou can put anything in the crazy slime!

S lime will not make you feel better if you eat it.

L imes are in the crazy slime.

I like slime so much.

M ake slime with a bicycle.

E at slime never!

Nancy Costa Cupe (7)
St Philip's CE Primary School, Odd Down

When I Grow Up

"Tia! Where's my new lipstick?" calls my mum.
"Have a look in my rucksack," I say, glum.
Mum said I couldn't wear lipstick today!
All I was doing was going out to play.
I hear Mum coming, *boom, boom, boom!*
"Put my make-up bag back and tidy up your room!"
I can't wait till I get my own make-up,
When I grow up.

Tia Louise Watts (7)
St Philip's CE Primary School, Odd Down

Candy Land

Fall down the rabbit's hole and the wonders you'll dream.
Candy Land smells of chocolate trees and cream.
I live in a candy tree house in South Africa.
I can see birds sing and hears elves talking.
Candy tastes like chocolate chips.
The soft gooey chocolate smells like fudge and custard creams.
When I touch it, it feels hot, creamy and it smells delicious.

Sophie Holborn (8)
St Philip's CE Primary School, Odd Down

Megladon Ride

M arvel at the size of the ancient beast
E very second feels like one minute
G oing as fast as a rocket
L and is far in the distance
A drenaline rushing through my body
D on't fall off, don't let go
O n the megladon's back, it feels slippery and scaly
N ow we've arrived at the tropical island!

Zach Turner (7)
St Philip's CE Primary School, Odd Down

Lucas The Spider

There is a young spider called Lucas,
Who lives in a house full of mucus.
He has a giant friend named Spotty,
Who is big, stinky and snotty.
Cheesy bananas is what Spotty eats,
Lucas is fast and creepy as he roams the streets.

Lewis James Mitchell (7)
St Philip's CE Primary School, Odd Down

Trapped Under

It all begins with your tiny little fingers,
It also painfully lingers,
It very much won't make you happy,
It doesn't happen to babies cos they have a nappy!
It has a hole in the middle,
When it happens, people shout, "Oh fiddle!"
The contents aren't neat,
So never trap your fingers under the toilet seat!

Louis Knight (9)
St Philip's CE Primary School, Odd Down

Magical Unicorn

U nder the cotton candy trees, the beautiful unicorns lie

N o clouds in the sky

I n chocolate rivers they swim

C louds melt in the sunlight

O h, how lovely they are

R un, run

N o stopping unicorns

D ays and days unicorns play

A nd have fun

Y ay!

Sara Maria Faur (9)

St Philip's CE Primary School, Odd Down

Silly Dog

The dog, the dog, the silly, silly dog,
He bounced on a bouncy trampoline,
He saw a wonderful cake and ate it,
He took it from a granny,
He was such a crazy dog,
He loved to play with other dogs.

Emmanuelle Maria Sasarman (7)
St Philip's CE Primary School, Odd Down

My New House

My new house is big and large,
It has three bedrooms and a great big yard,
It's closer to school, no time to be late,
But what's that noise?
Oh no, it's the bell for school, I'm going to be late!

Calum Willcox (9)
St Philip's CE Primary School, Odd Down

Christmas Eve

On Christmas Eve, I made a wish,
To get the biggest, best gift,
Then I tried to stay awake,
So Santa I would not miss,
I awoke with a bang and a shake,
I crept downstairs and there he was eating cake,
The biggest and best gift he gave to me,
Because he said I still believe.

Liam John Quintin (10)
St Philip's CE Primary School, Odd Down

Clean!

What could I see through my eye?
Was it a bird or a butterfly?
Or was it a van driven by a man?
Or was it a plane flying in the rain?
Was it a bunny eating honey?
Or a bear sitting on a chair?
So then I sat, getting shirty,
Then I realised my glasses were dirty!

Taliah Kathryn Johnson (10)
St Philip's CE Primary School, Odd Down

Mysterious Minecraft

M aking castles
I nventing a zombie man
N ever - the land you don't visit
E njoying building your worlds
C reating costumes
R ainbow homes
A lways fun
F ighting unicorns
T ravelling to other lands.

Amelia Offler (7)
St Philip's CE Primary School, Odd Down

Bendy's Life

I have a friend named Bendy,
He lives in a big house with his girlfriend, Wendy,
Sometimes they play games,
Which can be such a shame,
Because their house gets rather messy.

Eden Lawbuary-Stock (7)
St Philip's CE Primary School, Odd Down

Searching In Wonderland

A lice in Wonderland
"**L** ate, late, I'm late," says the White Rabbit
I n through the little door is a garden
"**C** an you swim, Alice? The house is flooded?"
E verybody has fun.

Sofia Mutlow (7)
St Philip's CE Primary School, Odd Down

Hidden Treasure

G ems that glow
O ver the rainbow
L ook and find them
D iscover the sparkles!

R ace for treasure
I n further we go
N uggets of gold
G ifts for pirates!

William McIvor (8)

St Philip's CE Primary School, Odd Down

Shark's Football

S hark's playing football.

H ear the crowd singing.

A t half-time, Shark drinks juice.

R ed card, but not for Shark.

K icking with his fin.

S coring the winning goal.

Riley Joyce (8)
St Philip's CE Primary School, Odd Down

Kittens

K is for kind
I is for intelligent
T is for ticklish
T is for troublesome
E is for always eating
N is for naughty
S is for silly.

Max Lakey (7)
St Philip's CE Primary School, Odd Down

Unicorns And Kittens

Unicorns and kittens are my favourite things,
When I see them together, they make me want to sing,
Cute and magic, adorable too,
I wish I could keep both of you.

Molly Coles (8)
St Philip's CE Primary School, Odd Down

My Magic Car

My brown Qashqai
My mid-range car
My magic button
I can fly so far
Up to the moon
Around the stars
Then back home
In my wonderful car.

Juliet Usher (8)
St Philip's CE Primary School, Odd Down

Sisters

Sisters support,
Sisters give,
Sisters are angels,
Sisters are lovely,
Sisters never leave your friendship,
Sisters are well-loved.

Tayla Ward (8)
St Philip's CE Primary School, Odd Down

Unicorn Fantasy

I open my eyes and what do I see?
A big fluffy unicorn staring at me.

With eyes as bright as a twinkling star,
I can hop on her back and travel afar.

Her wings are as light as a silky feather,
They can flap and fly whatever the weather.

The swishing tail glistening in the breeze,
Galloping high and low through the trees.

I think I've found where I want to be,
Where I can laugh and smile while being me.

Amelia Dewey (10)
Voyage Learning Campus, Worle

Candy Land

I opened my eyes and what did I see?
A candyfloss tree staring back at me,
It was tall, it was fluffy and very sweet,
The place was amazing, who would I meet?
I looked up and saw a rabbit,
It was made of chocolate, I wanted to grab it,
It said to me, "There is a beast,
It's got the princess, he's taken her east,
She now lives in a castle up on the hill,
She lives right next to the big windmill."
Off I set to save the day,
The Mentos monster wouldn't be there to stay,
At the cola river, I filled a cup,
I reached the windmill and launched it up,
I heard a fizz, I heard a pop,
His reign of terror would stop,
We celebrated, they made me king,
Now I don't have to worry about a thing.

Rhys Murphy (11)
Voyage Learning Campus, Worle

My Dream

What can I see?
I can see a giant looking down at me.

What can I hear?
I can hear footsteps - they sound really near.

What can I smell?
I can smell a potion cooking down in the well.

What can I taste?
I can taste the potion - it tastes like waste.

What can I touch?
I can touch fire - the potion helps me so much.

Harley Pearce (10)
Voyage Learning Campus, Worle

Slippery, Slidey Slime

"Don't make a mess!"
Shouts my mum from the kitchen
"We won't!" I say with a giggle
Today is squishy, squashy slime day, great!
Yes! Squeezy, squeaky fun!

"Mix it up fast," says M-Jay
"Where is the eye wash?" shouts Melody, excitedly
"Hmm! It feels so gooey
What great fun!"

Soft, wet and sticky
"Can we put glitter in?"
M-Jay says, "Noo!"
He splats the slime on Mum's favourite shoes
Too late... Let's hope she doesn't notice
"Harmony... M-Jay... Melody!"
Oops... Grounded for a week
But what fun we've had!

Harmony Reed (11)
Voyage Learning Campus, Worle

My Sensory Dream

Lines of golden trees, lined up in threes.

Gold leaves on the trees, crashing in the breeze.
Golden chocolate dropping down, all the way to
the ground.

The chocolate drops turn into a chocolate slime
stream,
I can reach down and splash in it - oh what a
dream!

I dunk biscuits into the chocolate slime,
And I gobble them up as I finish my rhyme.

Jayden Boyd (10)
Voyage Learning Campus, Worle

My Nightmare

What can I see?
I can see knives being thrown at me.
What can I hear?
Nuclear bombs - they sound like they're near!
What can I smell?
Gas and smoke - I don't feel well.
What can I touch?
I can hold a grenade tight in my clutches.
What can I taste?
I have ash in my mouth - I don't like the taste.

Toby Williams (8)
Voyage Learning Campus, Worle

My Dream

What can I see?
I can see a moving book with eyes...
It makes me feel curious.

What can I hear?
I can hear *tick-tock!* A clock...
It makes me feel nervous.

What can I smell?
I can smell lavender...
It makes me feel sleepy.

What can I touch?
I feel puffy slime...
It makes me feel calm.

What can I taste?
I can taste fruit - mango is the best...
It makes me feel excited.

When I wake up, I feel hungry and ready to explore.

Kyros Alabaf (9)
Voyage Learning Campus, Worle

Candy Land

I opened my eyes and what did I see?
A big, big candyfloss tree.

I opened the gate with all my might,
And on the other side, I had a fright.

I saw a bunny,
He was made out of honey.

He hopped away,
I wanted him to stay.

I went through the woods,
As quick as I could...

I really wanted to stay,
I hoped that was okay.

Rhys Jefferies (9)
Voyage Learning Campus, Worle

Slime

My slime is very nice, it runs through my fingers like a dice.
When I stretch it out wide, it looks glittery and wonderful.
It pops in my hand like bubble wrap, my friends open my draw and snap the glittery slime like bubble wrap.

Harry Dobbing (9)
Voyage Learning Campus, Worle

The Fat Cow

There was a cow that was very fat,
But he didn't realise that,
The farmer had in mind to kill,
And use the money to pay a bill.

James Pearce (10)
Voyage Learning Campus, Worle

The Creature

Soaring through the sky,
A majestic creature flies,
Over beautiful mountains and views,
Never missing a beat, the powerful wings fly on,
There's a determined look on the creature's face,
Who knows where it's going?
Through storm clouds and lightning bolts,
On and on it goes,
Where is it going?
Who does it know?
Nobody knows,
Still flying through the air at night,
On and on it goes.

Romilly C (10)
Weston All Saints Primary School, Weston

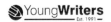
The Day I Flew Around The Sun On A Giant Waffle

I was lying in my garden one day,
When a giant waffle came to play.
He had a bowler hat and a curly moustache,
Which was orange and blue and was rather large.
He said to me, "Come on, get on,
Or we'll never make it round the sun.
We'll soar into space, just you and I!"
What could I say? I'd always wanted to fly!
So we zoomed out of the atmosphere,
The heat almost made me shed a tear.
"First stop!" he cried. "First up is the moon!"
So I had to abandon my funny cartoon.
We jumped down and floated around,
It made a hilarious twanging sound.
Up next was Mars where we played with a robot,
After, came Jupiter where we laughed a lot.
Then came Saturn and all the rest,
Which put my flying skills to the test.

Finally oh finally, we reached the sun,
I'd like to say it was lots of fun.
But that would be a lie,
The heat was why.
Anyway I said, "I'm tired, let's go!"
And the waffle and I, we flew back home to bed.

Lydia Shearman (11)
Weston All Saints Primary School, Weston

The Broccoli Bear

In the jungle, the jingly jangly jungle,
There, right there, on the fresh, tidy, clean trees,
Smells are spreading through the jingly jangly
jungle broccoli trees,
Roar!
Roar!
The sprinkle speckled bear in the jingly jangly
jungle,
On the fresh, tidy, clean broccoli trees,
He climbs like a monkey from branch to branch,
Gigantic grassy bear wriggles and shakes the trees
and,
Boom!
And that is the tale of the broccoli bear.

Reilly M (10)
Weston All Saints Primary School, Weston

Something Weird

I went to school today,
Something weird happened,
The school was quiet,
I went inside and nothing was in sight.

When I turned around,
I heard a cluck,
And saw a great big fat chicken sitting on the
floor,
I stared with astonishment.

I woke up with a jolt,
I knew it was just a silly dream,
I went to school today,
Now something weird has happened...

Edward H (10)
Weston All Saints Primary School, Weston

Magic Candy Land

The clouds are made of candyfloss
as they are the boss.
Rainbows made out of rainbow belts
and they melt.

As the sun melts them away
they show me the right way.
I fall on a marshmallow
it feels like a pillow.

As I pick up a sweet
and eat away as they say.
I don't realise it is Yemiah
as tiny as a sweet.

Up on a mountain
where there's a chocolate fountain.
With lollipop goats
and sugar sprinkle boats.

Now that's where we live
baking with a sieve
in our magic candy land.

Mohima C (10)
Weston All Saints Primary School, Weston

A Picnic On The Moon

Having a picnic on the moon,
is not what you normally do,
with floating rugs,
and flying mugs,
it's quite hard to achieve,
with sausage rolls glued to the floor,
and sandwiches stuck on a plate,
it's almost impossible to complete,
with hovering forks,
and gliding knives,
it's hard to accomplish,
but all that effort is worth it,
for the view of the shooting stars.

Jack Cartwright (10)
Weston All Saints Primary School, Weston

A Picnic In A Swamp

Crocodile teeth and fish eyes,
Frog liver and hippo pies,
Mosquito legs and rat claws,
Mudskipper legs and tusks of boars,
Bird feathers and piranha fins,
Plant broth and capybara chins,
Stick chips and mashed petals,
Tree sap and stewed nettles.

Andrew Docton (10)
Weston All Saints Primary School, Weston

YOUNG WRITERS INFORMATION

We hope you have enjoyed reading this book – and that you will continue to in the coming years.

If you're a young writer who enjoys reading and creative writing, or the parent of an enthusiastic poet or story writer, do visit our website **www.youngwriters.co.uk**. Here you will find free competitions, workshops and games, as well as recommended reads, a poetry glossary and our blog. There's lots to keep budding writers motivated to write!

If you would like to order further copies of this book, or any of our other titles, then please give us a call or visit **www.youngwriters.co.uk**.

Young Writers
Remus House
Coltsfoot Drive
Peterborough
PE2 9BF
(01733) 890066
info@youngwriters.co.uk

Join in the conversation!
Tips, news, giveaways and much more!

 **YoungWritersUK**    **@YoungWritersCW**